CONTENTS

- 2   The Cat at my House
- 4   Our Morning Meander
- 6   Doors
- 9   Miracle Cat
- 10   A Cat in Hatching Season
- 13   The Musical Cat at my House
- 15   Surprised
- 16   Cat Naps
- 19   Turf Wars
- 20   The Cat and the Weather
- 22   Triptych for a Semi-Sociable Cat
- 25   Her Name

THE CAT AT MY HOUSE

She's in the class of things I dote on,
right there with grandkids and backyard birds.
But I ache for accuracy when people speak of
"love bites" from cats. That's sugar coating.
Nothing like love informs those
dark echoes of the jungle.

People delight in describing the antics
of cats they think of as theirs. The cat at my house
plays games, too. Just let me sit down to read,
and she considers it my paramount duty
to give her a treat. Often as not
she'll swat the little biscuit across the room,
crouch chin to floor and creep up on it,
and pounce. Then launch an all-feet leap straight up
with a victory pirouette, and nonchalantly stroll away –
a playful predator.

JOSEPHINE

New Atlantic Media
Chapel Hill, NC
2018

JOSEPHINE

LAURENCE AVERY

Poems:
Copyright © 2017 Laurence Avery.

Photos & Drawings:
Copyright © 2017 Patricia Lockwood Davis.

All Rights Reserved.

Cover Design by Patricia Lockwood Davis
Book Layout by Tim Hubbard
Printed in the United States of America

New Atlantic Media
Chapel Hill, NC

10 9 8 7 6 5 4 3 2 1

ISBN 978-0-9912927-4-5

She's also found it fun to jump to a counter
by the fridge and rake off magnetized things
on the door – photos, art work by grandkids,
travel souvenirs. When I hear a clatter
and tell her "down, get down," she obeys,
only to hide under a table till I walk by,
then dart out and bat at my pants fiercely,
a sure sign of what she'd like to do –
lay my leg open with her claws.

The cat at my house is as close to a wild thing
as you'd want to live with. The jungle stirs in her bones.
Add a zero to the weight of this eight pound kitty,
and you'd have to cage her up and ship her home.

Our Morning Meander

Trees out her window are askitter with squirrels.
Rabbits nibble in the high grass.
People walk by, and when her window is up
speak to her as they pass.
Who could blame an indoors cat
for itching to be out and about in all that.

She has her own opinion of the leash she must wear –
and wouldn't seem ladylike if you knew it.
But after a serious nap,
she can view it
in a broad-minded way: "For all his talk,
it is I who take my assistant for a walk."

Unlike her indoor world,
the world out of doors is big,
and full of sights and smells and noises.
Any sensible cat, before embarking,
will sniff the breeze, cock an ear –
"*this* morning, what's to check on out here?"

Before her *aide-de-camp* has a clue,
she spots a twitch in the pine straw thatch,
crouches, and pounces. Whatever is under there –
bug, worm, figment – she'll catch.
Foolishly, a rabbit hops by, ignorant
of *its* danger: "If only I didn't have to drag my attendant!"

People find a cat on a leash irresistible.
Let a neighbor walk by, male or female,
and the human must reach down to stroke
feline fur, whose proprietress will not fail
to sniff the pants leg and proffered fingers,
then amble off, feeling not the least need to linger.

Alas, the out of doors is no paradise.
The screech of a leaf blower is not to be borne.
And there's that mysterious racket when a man
rounds the corner all of a sudden
pulling a heavy tote-box rat-a-tat-tat.
You'd scamper, too, to be again an indoors cat.

Doors

For our Josephine it is a truism that
any door should open for a cat.
She'll request assistance first with a friendly *yow*,
but any delay brings an adamant *yowl*.

Strange things could lurk behind a door,
things a cat must without fail explore.
Take the bedroom closet, where Rachel's shoes
lie scattered. First, why would Rachel choose
to wear such things at all? For a cat, it's a riddle.
But since she does, it's more than middl[e] –
ing strange she wears only two, not four –
a downright mystery. Furthermore,
an enigma looms when she takes a different twosome
every day. It's more than Josephine can fathom.
Still, she persists and probes – despite insomnia –
this riddle wrapped in a mystery inside an enigma.

Then what to do on a Sunday afternoon –
tops for naps – when like a typhoon
a crowd arrives – talk, talk, talk,
and not a word for Josephine? Worst of all,
some are small, and shriek, and precipitously dart!
At such times Josephine is art-
ful in escaping to the closet where overcoats
are kept, which hang to the floor and promote,
in the securest nook, contemplation of a comment
she heard among the small ones: "If two's company,
three a crowd, what's four?" "The only number
you spell," one yells, "with letters of a corresponding
number!" Josephine loses interest a.s.a.p.,
yawns, curls herself into a ball, and falls asleep.

Then there is that cabinet in the corner.
Nothing in it, you'd think, to cause a cat to stir.
Josephine has explored it often enough.
It never changes – an old computer and stuff
she wonders why her attendants even keep.
But still the cabinet doors are shut, and peep
behind them Josephine must. Why? A matter
of principle – as when a general marches
through conquered land just to show he can –
or abstractly put, to assert a fundamental feline
right to enter any door she pleases.

In this land where everyone seizes
                              opportunity,
where cats are poster pets for an open door policy,
all portals they approach should activate immediately.

Miracle Cat

If you have lived with a cat, you know
what I mean when I say the one at my house
can fly, walk on a cloud, even flow through key holes.

It has to count as flying when, from the floor,
she lands in the topmost nest of her kitty tower –
as high as the top of a door.

And it can't be harder to walk on a cloud
than to stroll atop a chair-back slat,
or pick your way through upright lipstick tubes
on Rachel's dresser like an acrobat.

Maybe not a key hole, but if you shut the bathroom door
and don't click it, you'll see it budge without fail,
then a nose and two round eyes, then
pointed ears, then a whole cat with high-rise tail.

A Cat in Hatching Season

Of course Jo-Jo hates the leash,
but has learned she can't go outside
without it. One morning she sniffed an egg shell,
not splattered as fallen from a nest, but divided

chippingly as when a hatchling frees itself.
The shell's coloration (white with end spots)
and location (under low branches)
suggested a towhee. Jo-Jo moved on at a trot.

From a dogwood a red blur shot
at her head. She saw the cardinal coming
and leaped within inches of the swooping bird,
front paws up slapping, clawing –

close to a clash. I couldn't spot a nest,
though one had to be close by, with three or four
nestlings – when parents are most aggressive.
But Jo-Jo was pulling toward a neighbor's back door,

where, in a cleared spot beneath a maple,
two fledgling bluebirds flailed their wings
with little to show for it. One managed to soar
the height of a chair seat. The other couldn't spring

that high. Spotting Jo-Jo, the parents
hopped about in the low branches, wings spread,
scolding loudly. Jo-Jo strained at the leash.
Had she been loose, two fledglings were surely dead,

perhaps an adult or two as well. So,
my little predator can make complaint,
but she doesn't live in the jungle and gets fed every day
from a can. Civil society requires restraint.

The Musical Cat at my House

All I know is what I see her do.
She's never undecided about the music.
Some composers leave her cold; some click.
Her tastes are limited. Play Beethoven, on cue
she skedaddles – his banging fortissimos
must hurt her ears. And Bach brings her no cheer.
Perpetual motion in his music makes her
antsy. She'll yawn, stretch out long, and bow
her back, then off she marches. Mozart holds her
a while. Like everyone, she finds him sublime,
but then wanders away, no doubt missing the purr
of his progressions. But something in Chopin chimes
with her kitty heart. A polonaise and, lickety-split,
here she comes running to sit, sit, sit.

Surprised

My roof is a playground for squirrels. Chasing
up the pines front and back, or the holly at the side,
they continue the game all over the roof,
then scramble down a tree for a tumble in the grass.

Soon back, they make a real racket atop the sunroom,
annoying Jo-Jo, who rates that room with wraparound windows
the heart of her turf. She'll glare at the ceiling
minutes on end, bristling at the clicking claws.

A while back, though, we were on the edge of a hurricane.
No real damage, just a blow that emptied the pines
of spent needles, leaving everything buried in brown thatch –
walk, yard, roof. Next day Jo–Jo and I,

out for a stroll, watched two squirrels jump
from the holly onto the roof, one after the other,
only to discover this time their claws were no match
for the thatch as slowly they slid toward the gutter, and over.

Such falls are nothing to squirrels, but sliding and falling
weren't what they expected when they jumped,
and the difference between expectation and what happened
was in the direction of bad – and a rude awakening.

Cat Naps

At my house the people
have one place to sleep;
the cat, five –
until she commandeered a sixth.

She's always had
a plump red pillow
in the bedroom
for all night snoozes,

a corner of the green
crushed velvet sofa
in the living room
for a late morning doze,

high and low nests
on her tower in the sun room
for afternoon naps
and a little bird watching,

and a cushy cat bed
in the family room
for early evening beauty rest
while her people watch tv.

You might think
that's enough places to sleep.
If you do,
you don't know cats.

One night Rachel,
retiring late,
laid her bathrobe
across a bedroom chair –

warm fleecy bathrobe stuff.
Next morning
it was the nest
for a curled up cat.

Now that nest
is the spot of choice
for all-nighters
and late morning naps.

Three times she circles,
then curls herself down,
tail over nose,
her mien proclaiming *what bliss!*

A few days into the new routine,
when I suggested we reclaim the robe,
Rachel's response was swift: "Oh,
we can't inconvenience the cat."

Turf Wars

The other day
I was making bread
at the kitchen counter,
and twice, with floured hands,
had returned miss cat to the floor,
which she grumbled about
because down there
she could see my moving arms
but not my kneading hands.

A third time she jumped to the counter.
A third time I set her back on the floor,
and this time thought
she'd gone off in a huff –

until I turned to get a bowl
and saw her atop the fridge
eyeing everything I did
in this quarter of her queendom.

The Cat and the Weather

Yowls, yips, pacings about –
every morning, no matter the weather,
Jo-Jo pesters me to take her out.
When finally my shoes are tied and I get
the leash, she sidles up for the chore
of getting hooked up – no threat
of tooth or claw. As soon as I open the door,
out she darts. But if the temperature
is near freezing, she will explore
no farther than the porch. Quickly she looks
back and paws at the door to help me open it.
We won't have been out as long as it took
to put on my coat. In cold weather
her world is incomplete
without central heat.

Warm weather is different – long walks
up the block to the yard where a woman throws out
seed, letting Jo-Jo stalk
birds and squirrels; down the hill to the big rocks,
where she can prowl ajuga jungles for voles
and worms and frogs – and muddy her socks.
Finally, she'll agree to be led
back in because that's when she gets fed.

This morning, the usual antics.
Putting on my coat, I told her it would be
another quick trip – thermometer stuck
at twenty degrees, over night
our first snow. Four inches of new white
on the yard. But once on the porch

Jo-Jo stared at the strange sight,
then glided down the porch
to a beam covered with snow.
Hopping up, she patted the stuff,
then sniffed it before venturing out, a row
of paw prints in the wake of her walk. *Enough*,
I thought, *This won't last long, not
with snow between her toes.* And she did
jump down – only to trot
along the edge of the porch making flurries
slapping snow off hellebore leaves.
A new world indeed. She hurried
to a spot covered with blown
white powder, and while I froze,
she crouched there to think
like a little sphinx.

Triptych for a Semi-Sociable Cat

1.

Jo-Jo slips into Rachel's dream
and, circling, nestles in her lap.
How cozy, Rachel thinks, as she
strokes the little neck and back
and warms to the purring. In the dream
she is wondering why this never happens
during the day, when little foot steps –
slowly the dream dissolves –
little foot steps on the covers
walking up her legs pry open
Rachel's eyes, to a pair
of pointed ears over two round eyes
peering down at her as if to say,
so here you are. Down the cat jumps
to her own red cushion bed on the floor –
for her, sharing a *room* is cozy enough.

2.

Anti-sociable she is with dogs.
In her worldview they are the bad guys –
big, little, no exceptions.
This morning she crouched
by a shrub, ready to attack
as a dog rounded the corner.
The white mutt bounced along,
happy to be out with its person,
tail wagging, blissful,
oblivious of the cat keeping its every step
under surveillance, and with narrowed eyes
thinking, *dogs are so dumb.*

3.

Outdoors, the crucial thing
is to get her bearings. Eyes
let Jo-Jo know if a dog is about;
ears, which birds are stirring.
But present conditions are a given.
The work is to ferret out the past
by sniffing hellebores off the porch
for a stray cat overnight,
and anemones by the walk
for nibbling deer late yesterday,
and pine needle thatch all round
for recent doings of our resident skink.
Never rushing into things,
she evaluates each current opportunity
in the light of enfolding history.

Her Name

Grandchildren helped us pick out Josephine
and find her name. "Skittles" was the first suggestion,
but that didn't fly – catchy, but only a candy.
Nothing about this cat suggests a snack food.

As they played with the kitten at the shelter,
another child thought "Feisty" might do.
That was closer, suggesting her energy,
but missed her natural dignity.

The quietest of the children was stroking the kitten
and smiling as the kitty rubbed the side of her head
against the girl's knee. "In school," the girl said softly,
"we're learning about Napoleon, and this little cat
is so regal she makes me think of his Empress."

The Poet

Laurence Avery had a decades-long career as teacher and scholar at UNC-Chapel Hill, where he served as chairman of the English department. He has published numerous articles on British and American playwrights and six books, among them; *A Southern Life: Letters of Paul Green, 1916-1981*, winner of the C. Hugh Holman Award for distinguished contributions to the study of Southern literature. Avery also published the definitive edition of Paul Green's play, *The Lost Colony*.

In 2006 Dr. Avery received the North Carolina Literary and Historical Association's R. Hunt Parker Award for significant contributions to North Carolina literature.

In 2013, Avery published his first book of poems, *Mountain Gravity*. The poems, accessible and erudite at once, touch the reader with historical stories of American Indians who lived in the North Carolina mountains, of contemporary Southern families maturing in a fast paced world, and of Carolina flora and fauna, beloved by Avery, adapting to changing habitats in the Blue Ridge Mountains.

The Artist

Naturally curious, **Patricia Lockwood Davis** took advantage of opportunities to study art at institutions in Boston, New York and Washington, DC and with several talented and creative artists in Ottawa, Boston, and Chapel Hill. Loving variety, she explored art education, art history, calligraphy, design, needlework, silk screening, weaving, figure drawing & portrait painting. Her preferred media include tempera, pen & ink, colored pencil, watercolor and acrylics.

In 2013, Patricia received a Certificate in Botanical Art and Illustration from the NC Botanical Garden and is a member of the Guild of Natural Science Illustrators. She has taught art in schools and privately in New York, Connecticut and Massachusetts and her art has been exhibited in Boston and Chapel Hill and their surrounding areas. Patricia now lives in Chapel Hill, NC.

One of her favorite quotes is Marcel Proust's "The real voyage of discovery is not in seeking new lands but in seeing with new eyes".

www.ingramcontent.com/pod-product-compliance
Lightning Source LLC
Chambersburg PA
CBHW070443010526
44118CB00014B/2173